THE PRACTICAL
ASTROLOGER

TABLE 4 ADDITION FOR HOURS		
Hours	1–2	Nothing
	3–9	1 m
	10–12	2 m

ABOVE Astrology was used in mediaeval times to diagnose illnesses and determine the best time for treatment. Chaucer's "Doctour of Phisick" (for example) "was grounded in astronomye" (= astrology). In this 16th-century engraving, astrologers are casting a birth chart for the child being born to the woman in the foreground.

the Earth rotates, and the timing of the movements of the astrological planets is calculated by their positions against the background of the stars, not by their places relative to Earth (the observer would have to be away from the Earth somewhere in space to see that). The fixed stars are so far distant from the solar system that they do not appear to move at all in relation to it. This means that the time taken for a fixed star to travel from directly overhead at midnight on one night to directly overhead at midnight the next night (which is 360° of the Earth's spin) never varies and is the time accepted by students of the heavens as the standard. It is this star or sidereal time, very slightly different from terrestrial time, that is used in astronomy, astrology and navigation for plotting the positions of the heavenly bodies. The distance between Earth and a fixed star is so immense that the same fixed star will appear to be directly overhead at midnight for millenia of centuries of human observation.

Sidereal time, like solar time, is divided into 24 hours with the same divisions of hours into 60 minutes and minutes into 60 seconds. But the sidereal hour is ten seconds longer than the solar hour, and this has to be borne in mind when converting solar time into sidereal time.

Sets of tables make the calculation of sidereal time simple. We begin with Table 1, which gives the sidereal time at midnight December31/January 1 for the years 1890 to 2000 AD. Table 2 gives the addition in hours and minutes to be made for the month; Table 3 for the day of the month. The first day of the month, being the operative day, is not included. Table 4 gives the addition for each hour.

To show how to calculate sidereal time, let us take as an example a baby whose umbilical cord was cut at 9.00 pm on 29 December, 1958.

Sidereal time for January 1, 1958	06.41
Addition for month (common year)	21.57
Addition for day	01.50
Addition for hour	00.02
TOTAL	29.50

Since we have to have a time that fits within 24 hours – or, to look at it another way, since 29.51 represents one day plus 5.51 hours – from any total that is more than 24 we subtract 24. The calculated sidereal time of the above birth is thus 5.51. It must be emphasized that the above calculation is merely to show how we arrive at sidereal time – it takes no account of the *place* where the baby was born. The only child of whom this calculation would be true would be one born at 0° of latitude and longitude, where the Greenwich meridian crosses the equator, and the infant would have first to see the light of day on a liner or possibly an aeroplane at a point in the Gulf of Guinea south of Ghana. To arrive at "corrected time," ie time corrected to take into account latitude and longitude, a number of other calculations have to be made.

Since daylight "travels" from east to west, dawn will be earlier in Europe than it is in England and later for an American than for a European. For a birth *east* of the Greenwich meridian four minutes for each degree of longitude east of the Greenwich meridian would need to be *added* to GMT. For a birth in the US four minutes of each degree of longitude *west* of Greenwich would have to be *subtracted*. Allowance for other anomalies such as Daylight Savings Time and, for example, the "mountain time" that is sometimes found in high living localities has also to be made.

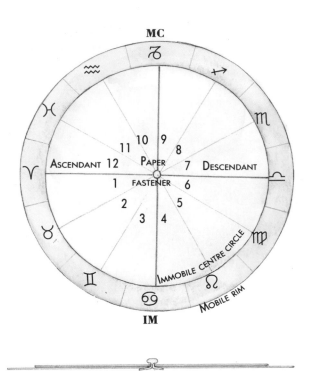

ABOVE A simple tool to make plotting charts easier: the inner circle with the houses marked on it is joined by a paper fastener to another, larger circle, on the rim of which the zodiac is marked.

A USEFUL SHORTCUT

If the astrologer is planning to erect a number of horoscopes, there is a useful piece of apparatus that he can make for himself. From a piece of stiff card cut a circle of a convenient size to act as a basic chart. If it is possible to mark all the 360° on the circumference, so much the better, but at least every five degrees round the whole circle should be marked as accurately as possible. On this draw a horizontal line ending in the ascendant to the east at the left hand and the descendant to the west at the right. If it is intended to use the Equal House system, the circle can be divided by radii into segments of 30° each, numbered for quick reference 1 to 12, the first being that from 9 o'clock to 8 o'clock, the second from 8 o'clock to 7 o'clock, and so on round the circle.

Superimpose the circle on a larger piece of card and mark out a larger circle on this with the same centre as the first. This is cut out in its turn; it will fit round the first like a tyre round a wheel. The two circles are held together by a paper fastener inserted through their common centre and the larger one moved round the smaller as required.

The larger circle is then also divided into twelve segments of 30° each and the signs of the zodiac are written anti-clockwise on the segments in their order – Aries, Taurus, Gemini, Cancer, Leo, Virgo, Libra, Scorpio, Sagittarius, Capricorns, Aquarius and Pisces. By turning the outer circle clockwise, Aries will rise above the eastern horizon, followed by Taurus and the rest. Thus the student, having discovered what sign is in the ascendant at the time of the event being charted, can move the outer circle to the appropriate position.

He can then cut out ten small pieces of card, each with a pointer protruding from one side, on each of which he draws the symbol of one of the planets. These can be stuck on top of a drawing pin. The pointer is used to indicate the exact degree of the planet's position on the chart – not always easy to point to by the symbols themselves, which are large enough to stretch over several degrees of any circle that can be drawn on an average-sized sheet of paper. With this simple apparatus the astrologer has literally at his fingertips all the elements he needs to plot his charts.

FROM CALCULATION TO INTERPRETATION: THE SIX ELEMENTS

Let us now erect a horoscope for a woman born at Harrow, England, at 1.30 am on July 2, 1951. Following is a résumé of the steps we have to take for the completion of the whole chart and its interpretation.

1. Calculate the sidereal time of birth.

2. From this we find the positions of the signs of the zodiac at the time of birth.

3. From an ephemeris for the year 1951 plot the positions of the planets on the horoscope.

4. To interpret the horoscope we first look at the relationships of the planets to the signs. The zodiacal signs have all been given their own characteristics by astrologers down the ages, as have the planets (see Chapters Two and Three), so a specimen horoscope may have the Sun in Aquarius, the Moon and Mercury in Capricorn, Venus in Pisces, Mars in Sagittarius and Jupiter in Leo, all of which give combinations of characteristics. Taken as a whole, they may complement or contradict each other (which is to be expected, because human beings are a mass of potentials, some of which may be fulfilled at the expense of others. There are contradictions and inconsistencies in the characters of all of us.)

HOW TO CALCULATE SIDEREAL TIME

The calculation of the sign of the zodiac rising at the moment of birth – and the consequent position of the other signs and of the planets – relies upon a geocentric view of the universe. For this reason, adjustments have to be made to the 'terrestrial' time of birth to find the 'sidereal' (or star) time. Though it may look daunting at first, the mathematics is very simple and is standard for all birth charts. Do one, and you can do them all. We have chosen Marilyn Monroe as an example to follow.
Marilyn Monroe was born at 9.09 am, June 1, 1926, local time Los Angeles.

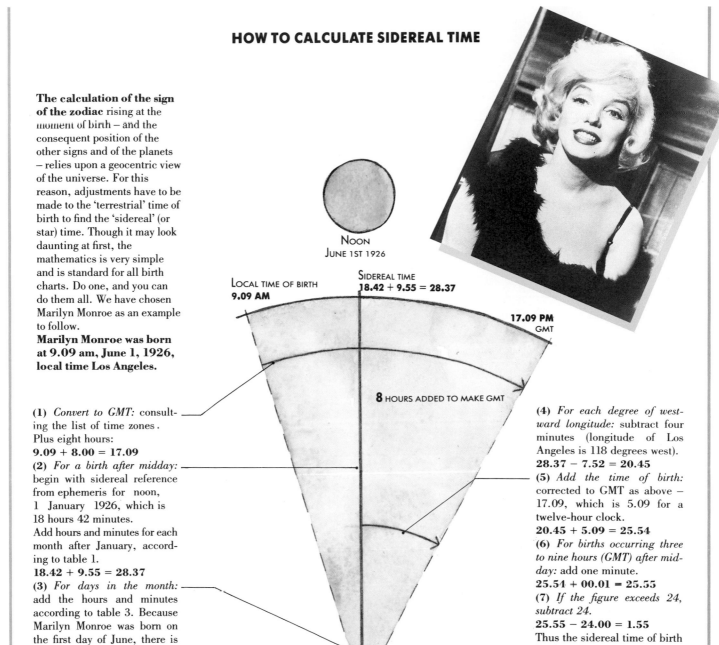

NOON
JUNE 1ST 1926

LOCAL TIME OF BIRTH
9.09 AM

SIDEREAL TIME
18.42 + 9.55 = 28.37

17.09 PM
GMT

8 HOURS ADDED TO MAKE GMT

(1) *Convert to GMT:* consulting the list of time zones.
Plus eight hours:
9.09 + 8.00 = 17.09
(2) *For a birth after midday:* begin with sidereal reference from ephemeris for noon, 1 January 1926, which is 18 hours 42 minutes.
Add hours and minutes for each month after January, according to table 1.
18.42 + 9.55 = 28.37
(3) *For days in the month:* add the hours and minutes according to table 3. Because Marilyn Monroe was born on the first day of June, there is nothing to add.

(4) *For each degree of westward longitude:* subtract four minutes (longitude of Los Angeles is 118 degrees west).
28.37 − 7.52 = 20.45
(5) *Add the time of birth:* corrected to GMT as above – 17.09, which is 5.09 for a twelve-hour clock.
20.45 + 5.09 = 25.54
(6) *For births occurring three to nine hours (GMT) after midday:* add one minute.
25.54 + 00.01 = 25.55
(7) *If the figure exceeds 24, subtract 24.*
25.55 − 24.00 = 1.55
Thus the sidereal time of birth for the subject is 1.55.

LEFT Portents in the sky in past ages caused consternation. Here the populace show wonder and fear at an eclipse of the sun and astrologers calculate its significance.

1. Find the position of Mars at 6.00 am GMT on March 5, 1965. 6.00 am GMT on March 5 is 6 hours plus 10 seconds per hour sidereal time before noon on that day = 6 hours, 1 minute

Noon position of Mars, retrograde, on March 4, 1965

20   41.2

Noon position of Mars, retrograde, on March 5, 1965

20   18.2

Difference for 24 hours   23.0

Difference for 6 hours 1 minute (by calculator, calculation by logs could also be used)   5.8

Required position (20   18.2 +   5.8)   20   24.0

2. Find the position of Mars at 6.00 pm GMT on March 4, 1965. As above, the difference for 6 hours, 1 minute sidereal time is 5.8

Subtract this from the noon position of Mars on March 4:

20   41.2 − 5.8   20   35.4

(Note that in the figures above seconds are given as decimal fractions of a minute)

In an ephemeris table all the times following the symbol R are retrograde until D (for "direct") appears in the column – this marks the turning point when the planet has resumed or will resume direct motion.

FORECASTING THE FUTURE

Astrology uses transits and progressions as time-tables for the future. Transits are movements of the planets which are indicated by formulae such as T♃☌☿, meaning, 'transiting Jupiter in conjunction with Mercury.' The transit is interpreted according to whether the planets are within the orb of conjunction and advancing towards its completion or moving away from each other after total concurrence, the former indicating an increasing interaction of both planets' potencies, the other their diminishing. There are also certain key-spots, the ascendant and the MC for example, on which planets are said to exert greater influence as they pass over them. Astrologers claim that times of opportunity or menace in a life can be indicated by a comparison of planet transits on a day years ahead, obtained from an ephemeris, with the position of the heavenly bodies on the natal chart. The type of event to be expected may also be indicated. One can see a promise or threat approaching, watch it happening and observe it modifying, like weather systems on a film. An astrological principle is that the natal horoscope must never be contradicted, nor can one ever certainly foretell how an individual will react to promised wealth or threatened woe.

The student looking for future trends consults an ephemeris for the relevant day and notes the aspect of every planet in turn with each natal planet. Next, he notes the relationships of the transiting planets with the houses – in the case of fast-moving planets as accurately as possible by interpolation – and then summarizes his findings.

Progressions are daily positions of the planets after the day of birth plotted according to a formula of 'a day for a year'. The positions of planets and signs twenty days after a birth allegedly give an approximation of trends occurring in the subject's twentieth year, thirty days after of happenings in the thirtieth year, etc. Progressions are calculated proportionately, one day to a year, 12 hours to six months, one hour to 15 days, four minutes to one day and one minute to six hours. For exact work, calculate in days.

For the many who do not know their hour of birth, a 'flat'

EXAMPLE: Forecast the astrological conditions at midday on 27th June, 1991, for a subject born at 14.53 on 13th October, 1963

	YEARS	MONTHS	DAYS	HOURS	MINUTES
Hours and minutes after the birth on 13th October until midnight				9	7
Days from 13th until end of October			18		
Months from October till end of 1963		2			
Years from 1964 to 1990	27				
Months in 1991 till end of May		5			
Days till 26th June			26		
Hours on 27th June till midday				12	
TOTAL	27	8	14	21	7

(30 days from the 'Days' column are carried forward as 1 Month)

Progression Calculations 27 years = 27 days; 8 months = 16 hours; 14 days = 1 hour, 56 minutes; 21 hours = 3½ minutes; 7 minutes is too small to be included.

Total: 27 days, 18 hours to the nearest hour. Adding 27 days 18 hours to the birth time we arrive at 08.53 on 10th November, when the sky will approximate to that

at noon on 27th June, 1991. (A calculation on a basis of 10,119 days between the above dates divided by 365¼, allowing for Leap Years, gives exactly the same result)

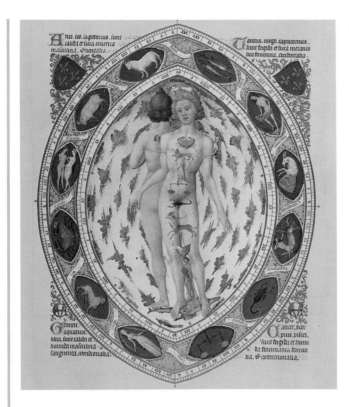

THE HOUSES

There are at least nine systems of plotting the divisions of the houses in a chart. A serious student of astrology needs to know them and the reasonings and calculations behind each and should study a specialist publication such as *House Systems Comparison*, which lists house cusps and gives the placement of the planets according to each system.

THE SIGNS

There are also differences in the spaces given to the signs which expand and contract according to their positions in the zodiac. The latitudes of the rising and setting of heavenly bodies are determined by the earth's tilt; from this arises the concept of signs of long ascension and short ascension, whereby some signs take longer to rise than others.

The simplest method is to use 30° divisions for both houses and signs, which provides horoscopes as adequate as those erected by other systems. The advanced student must, however, study every method and choose that which seems to him most accurate and effective.

TOP A zodiac from *Les Tres Riches Heures du Duc De Berry* showing the influence of the different constellations on the parts of the body.

LEFT An engraving showing Arab astrologers using early astronomical instruments.

BELOW An astrological chart of the northern hemisphere, showing the constellations, from the beautifully illustrated *Atlas Coelistis* of Andreas Cellarius.

chart may be drawn with 0° Aries at the ascendant and the planets placed at their noon positions on the birthday. This is too approximate to be satisfactory. The astrologer may make two or more calculations based on different times on the birthday and decide which of them suits his subject's character best, but this method is too subjective. A better way, known as 'rectification' is to erect a horoscope for the dates and times of great events in the subject's life (marriage, grave illness, change of career) and see which birth chart fits them best.

laughing at it and the protagonists in it, including themselves, and analyzes it intellectually. Gemini subjects take nothing seriously. So, in love, in spite of their temporary depth of feeling – for the intensity of involvement lasts only while it is new – they are superficial, light-hearted, cool, flirtatious and unimaginative in the understanding of the pain they may give others. They like intrigue, the excitement of the chase, but once they have caught the prey, they lose interest and look around for the next creature to pursue. In less serious situations they make witty, entertaining companions, good acquaintances rather than friends. Even at their worst they are never dull – there is usually playfulness below the surface, and they can be brilliant conversationalists – but they can also be quarrelsome, prattlers, boasters, liars and cheats.

Geminians can be successful in many walks of life though their general characters tend to make them unreliable. They are often skillful manipulators of language, in speech and writing, and may be debaters, diplomats (though in politics they are more interested in theory than practice), orators, preachers (brilliant rather than profound), teachers, authors and poets, journalists or lawyers. In business any work which combines quick-wittedness with change of surroundings suits them – working as a travelling salesman, brokerage work or dealing of any kind. Because they are dispassionate, logical, rational and analytical they make good scientists, especially medically, astronomers and mathematicians. They can also make excellent members of the Forces, for they take danger no more seriously than anything else and can earn themselves a reputation for devotion to duty and heroic acts. In the arts they may excel in music, painting and sculpture. They make good psychical researchers of a sceptical kind. Negatively they can degenerate into confidence tricksters, thieves and even adepts in the black arts.

Physically Geminians often appear youthful, even child-like. They have tall, thin, but strong and active, bodies, with long arms and legs culminating in short, fleshy hands and feet. Their faces are also inclined to be long and sallow, with large, piercing hazel eyes, often in contrast with dark complexions. Their hair is often dark, almost black. They use their eyes and hands expressively – they are great gesticulators – and their movements are quick and active.

Gemini rules the arms, shoulders, hands, lungs and nervous system and its subjects need to beware of diseases and accidents associated with the upper part of the body, as well as nervous and pulmonary disorders such as catarrh and bronchitis. Their mercurial nature may also affect a constitution which is usually not strong if it is put under strain.

ABOVE Sir Arthur Conan Doyle (1859–1930), born May 22. A many-sided character, he was active in public affairs, the creator of the astute, practical Sherlock Holmes, and a convinced Spiritualist.

† CANCER †

The Cancerian character is the least clear-cut of all those associated with the signs of the zodiac. It can range from the timid, dull, shy and withdrawn to the most brilliant, and famous Cancerians are to be found throughout the whole range of human activity. It is a fundamentally conservative and home-loving nature, appreciating the nestlike quality of a secure base to which the male can retire when he needs respite from the stresses of life, and in which the Cancerian woman can exercise her strong maternal instincts. The latter tends to like and to have a large family. "Nestlike" is an appropriate adjective for the Cancerian home, for its inhabitants tend to favour the dark, mysterious, but comfortable type of house which has something of the air of a den about it, a place which belongs to the family rather than existing as a showcase to impress visitors.

That is not to say that the Cancerian is unsociable, just that for him there is a time to socialize and a time to be solitary, and this is part of the apparent contradiction in his nature. Outwardly he can appear formidable – thick-skinned, unemotional, uncompromising, obstinately tenacious, purposeful, energetic, shrewd, intuitive and wise, sometimes with a philosophical profundity of thought verging on inspiration. His intimates, however, may see a very different character, one with a sympathetic and kindly sensitivity to other people, especially those he loves. He is able to identify with the situations of others because of the keenness of his imagination. He is often over-imaginative and prone to fantasy, sometimes trying to shape his life to fit some romantic ideal. He is appreciative of art and literature, and especially of drama, where the spectacle and ebb and flow of action and feeling particularly excite him. He may himself possess considerable literary, artistic or oratorical talent. His sharp ear and talent for mimicry can sometimes give him success on the stage, though his tendency to be emotional may make him overact. Interestingly – because he gives the impression of being down-to-earth – he is often fascinated by the occult and

is more open to psychic influence than the average. If he can reconcile the personal conflict of his urge to be outgoing with the reserve that causes him to withdraw into himself, then at his best he can inspire his generation, especially the youthful part of it, by his idealism. A job in which he could express this, and in which he could do well, would be as a leader in a youth organization.

In his personal relationships he is mentally a mixture of toughness and softness, often emotional and romantic to the point of sentimentality in his fantasies; but in real life and in his marriage, his loving is not sentimental but tenaciously loyal. Even if he has affairs (and he may do so, for the male in particular is open to sensual stimulation), his first loyalty remains to his wife and family, of whom he regards himself as the protector. Both the Cancerian man and woman love unreservedly, giving much and asking little in return – in fact one of the most important lessons they have to learn is to receive gracefully. They are too easily influenced by those

OPPOSITE Mike Tyson is an example of (in his own field) the "most brilliant" of Cancerians, and he is certainly "outwardly formidable," though not perhaps in the usual meaning of the term for the Cancer subject.

ABOVE This mid-fifteenth century French illustration of Cancer the Crab is rather more like a lobster. The reaper again represents an activity of the season, not of the sign.

they love or admire, and swayed by the emotion of the moment. They are also loyal friends, the negative side of their faithfulness being clannishness, the narrow patriotism of "my country right or wrong"; and closing ranks in suspicion and coldness towards outsiders.

Cancerians have a retentive memory, particularly for emotionally laden events which they can recall in detail for years afterwards. They are strongly governed by childhood memories and, since they live intensely in the past in memory and in the future in imagination, a chance meeting with someone for whom they had unrequited love, even if they thought they had conquered the feeling, will easily rouse the emotion all over again.

His abilities fit the Cancerian for a wide range of occupations. As he is interested in what people are thinking and able to judge what they can safely be told, he can be a good journalist, writer or politician, though in this last capacity he is more likely to remain in the background rather than attain prominent positions of power. He may, indeed, change his party. He can serve in other departments of public affairs, especially those which involve looking after others, for example in any kind of service from welfare and nursing to catering — his own love of comfort and good living makes the Cancerian an excellent chef or housekeeper. He sometimes has a penchant for trade or business and is often successful as a captain of industry. This is because he is an excellent organizer with a good sense of value and economy which he may combine with a flair for inventiveness and originality. The romantic side of his nature makes him enjoy grubbing about in places where exciting discoveries may be made (old stamp collections in attics in which there may be a twopenny-blue Mauritius worth thousands of pounds!), and if he can do this professionally as a secondhand dealer or specialist in antiques, he will be happy. More common occupations which suit some subjects of Cancer are an estate agent, gardener and sailor.

ABOVE Sarah Bernhardt (1844–1923), born October 22. This French actress, who performed throughout the world, was typically Libran in her successful theatre managements.

may feel if the two have had a tiff. Nor can the Libran's spouse often complain that he or she is not understood, for the Libran is usually the most empathetic of all the zodiacal types and the most ready to tolerate the beloved's failings.

The negative Libran character may show frivolity, flirtatiousness and shallowness. It can be changeable and indecisive, impatient of routine, colourlessly conventional and timid, easygoing to the point of inertia, seldom angry when circumstances demand a show of annoyance at least; and yet Librans can shock everyone around them with sudden storms of rage. Their love of pleasure may lead them into extrava-

ABOVE Franz Liszt (1811–1886), born October 22. He is pictured playing the piano for the Imperial Family in Vienna. Librans may find success as composers.

gance; Libran men can degenerate into reckless gamblers, and Libran women – extravagant, jealous and careless about money – sometimes squander their wealth and talents in their over-enthusiasm for causes which they espouse. Both sexes can become great gossipers. A characteristic of the type is an insatiable curiosity that tempts them to enquire into every social scandal in their circle.

In their work the description "lazy Libra" which is sometimes given is actually more alliterative than true. Librans can be surprisingly energetic, though it is true that they dislike coarse, dirty work. Although some are modestly content, others are extremely ambitious. With their dislike of extremes they make good diplomats but perhaps poor party politicians, for they are moderate in their opinions and able to see other points of view. They can succeed as administrators, lawyers (they have a strong sense of justice, which cynics might say could handicap them in a legal career), antique dealers, civil servants and bankers, for they are trustworthy in handling other people's money. Some Librans are gifted in fashion designing or in devising new cosmetics; others may find success as artists, composers, critics, writers, interior decorators, social workers or valuers, and they have an ability in the management of all sorts of public entertainment. Some work philanthropically for humanity with great self-discipline and significant results. Libran financiers sometimes make good speculators, for they have the optimism and ability to recover from financial crashes.

Physically the Libran has a well-proportioned, fundamentally strong physique of between average height and tall, and a round skull and face. The hair is often fair, smooth, and fine rather than curly; the complexion is good and the eyes often blue and very expressive.

RIGHT Bruce Springstein, born September 23, 1949. The Boss: a musician very different from Liszt but still a Libran!

Libra governs the lumbar region, lower back and kidneys. Its subjects must beware of weaknesses in the back, and lumbago, and they are susceptible to troubles in the kidneys and bladder, especially gravel and stone. They need to avoid over-indulgence in food and especially drink, for the latter can particularly harm the kidneys.

BELOW The more usual though more bizarre portrayal of Capricorn is to be seen in the roundel taken from an English Psalter, York, c1170.

ABOVE This naturalistic illustration of Capricorn from a mid-15th century French Calendar and Book of Hours is in marked contrast to the mythical creature with a goat's head and body and a fish's tail, usually knotted.

the corporate success which they had planned for their firms. They can spread gloom and tension in their circle which depresses everyone around them. In the extreme this trait can make them manic-depressive, ecstatic happiness alternating with the most wretched of misery for no reason that the subject of these emotions can name.

Their intellects are sometimes very subtle. They think profoundly though with little originality, have good memories and an insatiable yet methodical desire for knowledge. They are rational, logical and clear headed, have good concentration, delight in debate in which they can show off their cleverness by luring their adversaries into traps and confounding them with logic.

In their personal relationships they are often ill-at-ease, if not downright unhappy. They are self-centred, wary and suspicious of others, and in turn attract people who neither trust nor understand them. They prefer not to meddle with others nor to allow interference with themselves. Casual acquaintances they treat with diplomacy, tact and, above all,

ABOVE Elvis Aaron Presley (1935–1977), born January 8. "A strong attraction to music" is supposed to be a Capricornian characteristic, which understates the case somewhat for the King of Rock'n'Roll.

reticence. They make few good friends but are intensely loyal to those they do make, and they are bitter, revengeful enemies. They sometimes actively dislike the opposite sex and test the waters of affection gingerly before judging the temperature right for marriage. Once wedded, however, they are faithful, though inclined to jealousy. Family life, if well ordered as they like it to be, more than balances the goatlike inclination to lechery and inconstancy which some old authorities have ascribed to Capricorns.

Besides those already mentioned, faults to which the type is prone are over-conventionality, bigotry, selfishness, carelessness about personal appearance, avarice and miserliness, chronic complaining, incessant unnecessary worrying, and severity spilling over into cruelty.

Their occupations can include most professions that have to do with maths or money and they are strongly attracted to music. They can be economists, financiers, bankers, speculators, contractors, managers and also estate agents. They excel as bureaucrats, especially where projects demanding long-term planning and working are concerned, and their skill in debate and love of dialectic make them good politicians. They are excellent teachers, especially as principals of educational establishments where they have the authority to manage and organize without too much intimacy with the staff members. If working with their hands, they can become practical scientists, engineers, farmers and builders. The wit and flippancy which is characteristic of certain Capricornians may make some turn to entertainment as a career.

Physically they have thin bodies and are below average height, with lean, narrow chinned faces. The long skull, crowned with sparse black hair, sits on a scrawny neck, and moustache and beard are also thin. They are narrow chested and may be weak kneed, a handicap that gives them an ungainly bearing. In spite of their unprepossessing physique, Capricornians have a reasonably strong constitution. Many of the ailments of which they frequently complain – for they are inclined to hypochondria – are psychosomatic and due to their natural melancholia and depression.

Capricornus governs the knees, bones and skin, so its subjects may be liable to fractures and strains of the knees and other defects of the legs. Skin diseases from rashes and boils to leprosy (in countries where that disease is prevalent) are dangers, and digestive upsets may be caused by the Capricornian's tendency to worry or suppress emotions. Anaemia, Bright's disease, catarrh, deafness, rheumatism and rickets are also said to threaten the natives of this sign.

FAMOUS CAPRICORNS

Richard Nixon, born January 9, 1913. He possessed the Capricornian qualities of persistence, ambition for authority and attraction to a political career, and self-pity.

Louis Pasteur (1822–1895), born December 27. The French chemist and microbiologist, pioneer of vaccination, wrote, "will, work and success . . . fill human existence" – almost a Capricornian manifesto!

Sir Isaac Newton (1642–1727), born December 25. He was typically Capricornian in his mathematical genius and his secret interest in the occult (alchemy).

ABOVE Carl Gustav Jung (1875–1967) taught that there existed a collective subconsciousness of mankind. Astrology believes that this may be energized by the spiritual influence of the Sun.

RIGHT Symbolic representation of occupations connected with water with which the Moon is assocated. Above is Diana, the Moon goddess, holding a crescent, the planet's symbol. Her chariot wheel bears the sign of Cancer.

are sure intuition, delicacy of feeling, aesthetic receptivity and affection – especially within the family, between siblings, or for children by parents – for lunar love is nonsexual, chaste and often spiritual. Spiritual also is the intelligence the Moon bestows on its natives, since they use their experience of life to develop the reverential side of their characters and the sensitivity of their inner natures. Such characters will inevitably be introspective which is no bad quality provided that it is controlled. The lunar woman may well be an ardent feminist, proud of her sex and of the qualities belonging to it, yet deeply maternal and protective of her family. Both she and her male counterpart may have a strong sense of loyalty and patriotism.

Not such good qualities of the lunar character are its moodiness, restlessness – often expressed in arbitrary changes of mind and outlook – impressionability, impulsiveness, and tendency to join with the crowd in doing what everyone else is doing, following the fashion of the moment. The character's placidity can easily degenerate into passivity and timidity, or

become boring, as the aesthetic sensitivity may deteriorate into fantasy and dreaminess. There is also a risk that a Moon-man may develop a mother-complex.

The Moon is associated with water and its influence on the tides causes it to symbolize change and motion, though in a rhythmic rather than an anarchic fashion. Rhythm, both in the ebb and flow of the sea and the Moon's waxing and waning, is a symbol of pregnancy, while the conjunction of the Sun and new Moon signifies copulation. More generally, the Moon's cycle portrays the physical change of life, growth from birth to maturity followed by a gradual decay back into nothingness.

The planet also indicates astrologically the struggle, to be found in all human beings, between the flesh and the spirit, for the Moon is pulled in one direction by the Sun, symbolizing spirit, and in another by the Earth, portraying matter. This does not mean that the lunar character necessarily exhibits inconsistency to those who know him, and the appearance or not of the inner struggle depends largely on the position of the Moon in relation to other planets. A conjunction of Moon and Sun, for example, presents a subject who is exactly what he appears to be; but if Sun and Moon are opposed, the

ABOVE Until the discovery of Neptune, only the Moon was associated with the rivers and seas. The Moon's effect upon tides is obvious, and the transfer of supposed influence to the "new" planet provided excellent ammunition for the sceptic.

individual will see himself as possessing one kind of character while observers may see a quite different and even opposite type. If the Moon is in aspect (see page 23 for full explanation) with just one other planet, consistent conduct of one kind or another will appear, but if there are aspects between the Moon and many planets the result is a person who fits his or her behaviour to the company. If the Moon's influence is very prominent in a subject's horoscope it may be expressed in a way that is uncharacteristic of the delicacy, sensitivity and spirituality generally associated with the planet, going beyond these and causing him to call attention to himself in his profession, whatever that may be. Thus he may be an amusing entertainer, not afraid of exhibitionism if it raises a laugh, or a politician whose witty speeches, artfully worked at, could earn him advancement, especially if backed by the more solid lunar qualities.

Physiologically the Moon governs the autonomic system, with its numerous nervous reflexes and the automatic physical responses we develop from our birth. It also rules the stomach, womb, ovaries, breasts and pancreas. A faulty pancreas can give rise to emotional instability and, rightly or wrongly, the association of extreme weakness of this kind with the phases of the Moon has given rise to the word "lunatic" to describe

madness. The Moon also influences body fluids, the circulation of the blood and the digestive and lymphatic systems that nourish, protect and lubricate. In addition to its effect on human physiology, the Moon is supposed especially to influence plant growth.

Psychically the Moon represents the right-hand hemisphere of the brain, the seat of intuition. As the Sun deals with the universal subconsciousness, so the Moon is the planet of the individual subliminal mind and its psychological characteristics. It links present and past, with the result that lunar personalities yearn nostalgically for times that are gone. If, however, they are balanced in outlook, they will use their memories and past experience as an inspiration for future action. The Moon, cyclic and rhythmic in its own behaviour, forms habit patterns in its subjects which result from the ebb and flow of sensation in them and their emotional responses to these.

The Moon's symbol is a crescent which, as an incomplete circle, represents the mind, the visible crescent symbolizing the conscious mind, the invisible remainder of the circle the subconscious. It rules in Cancer, the night-time house, appropriately a water sign; its house is the fourth, its day Monday, its best hours the second, ninth, sixteenth and twenty-fourth.

BELOW The heavenly body with which we are on the most intimate terms: an Apollo 12 photograph of the lunar surface featuring the crater Erastosthenes, 38 miles in diameter.

ABOVE As this extraordinary 17th-century French illustration shows, the effect of the Moon upon women was seen as pretty drastic. Heaven knows what was supposed to happen at the full moon.

ABOVE The rhythm of the Moon's waxing and waning is symbolic of pregnancy.

MERCURY

Because it is closest to its parent Sun and the smallest in the solar system, Mercury is regarded as the planet of childhood and youth. It has the greatest lineal speed and shortest sidereal period and these give it a sprightliness in comparison with the other planets that both supports the idea of youth and explains why, in mythology, it was regarded as the nimble messenger of the gods who had wings on his feet that whisked him through the skies.

To be mercurial is to possess an impetuous intuition, to sparkle with ready wit and to be agile, volatile, changeable and restless. The Mercurian is liable to have a good memory and to be intelligent, even brilliant, one of those lucky people who can pass examinations without ever seeming to do a stroke of work or needing to do one. But although he is strongly intellectual, greedy for knowledge and capable of great learning, his scholarship is likely to be wide, not profound, for he lacks application and prefers to change to learning a new skill or science rather than be bored by the effort needed to deepen what he already knows. He is strongly rational and objective, remains uncommitted in doubtful matters, and will sit charmingly and innocuously on any fence he can find.

If he becomes an educationalist, he will be a good one, for he enjoys teaching and is able to communicate. His enthusiasm will also fire his pupils, though they may sometimes be shaken by his sudden outbursts of temper, and he will not suffer fools gladly. That ability to communicate allied with his gifts of self-expression in speech and writing can also gain him a reputation in advertising or the media, where he

A Roman face urn from the late 2nd century AD, dedicated to Mercury.

LEFT A vigorous representation of Neptune. His chariot is drawn by fish-tailed white horses and he is smiled upon by Juno, accompanied by her peacock.

personalities and despair resulting in suicide. Their favourite weapons in destroying themselves are overdoses of their customary sedatives, or poison gas.

Astrologers point out that Neptune was discovered within a couple of years of the foundation of the modern spiritualist movement, usually dated from the manifestation of psychic phenomena at the home of the Fox family in Hydesville, New York, in 1848. The century and a half since then has seen the development of considerable interest in the scientific investigation of occult phenomena (the Society for Psychical Research was founded in 1882) and of major world spiritual movements. These include Pentecostalism, named as a third force in Christianity after Catholicism and Protestantism, the charismatic movement, and ecumenicalism – not only within Christianity in the World Council of Churches, but between the other great religions of the Earth.

Before the discovery of Neptune the government of the seas, and liquids generally, had been assigned to the Moon, but was then transferred to the new planet – mistakenly, it may be argued, since the influence of the Moon on the oceans is obvious. Physiologically Neptune rules the thalamus – that part of the brain which controls the aural and optic nerves – and the rhythms of growth, the spinal canal and some nervous and mental processes. Its negative effects include hysteria, insanity, mental and emotional disturbances, neuroses and obsessions, together with mysterious illnesses which in our present state of knowledge cannot be diagnosed. Neptune is characterized by a trident, represented by a half-circle (the human mind) transcending the cross of matter. Its zodiacal sign is Pisces and it is connected with the twelfth hour.

PLUTO

Pluto, in its orbital period of 248 years, moves far too slowly to relate to individual signs of the zodiac and needs to be seen in the context of the whole horoscope. Pluto was the god of death and the underworld and the planet named after him is that of death and destruction, representing the dark side of mankind. Astrologers claim that the almost exact coincidence of its discovery in 1930 with the rise of the Nazis (its influence is also powerful in Hitler's horoscope) was no accident. They also point out that the 1930s saw the climax of racketeering in the USA, a great period of lawlessness, and that international gangsterism in the shape of Hitler, Mussolini, Stalin and Hirohito, and many lesser luminaries of that ilk, flourished at the same time. The period was also that in which international enterprises began to come into prominence – worldwide business cartels, superpower politics, and cross-border movements and action groups like the Third International, fascist philosophy and the Mafia, all breaking out of their original national confines. The realization of their power by the masses, including the unions, mass demonstrations and sometimes mass hysteria, as at the Nuremberg Rallies, all make Pluto a planet potentially to be feared. Its influence continues today in various subcultures and the worldwide

ABOVE Lenin (1870–1924) and Stalin (1879–1953), architects of the Russian revolution that replaced the imperial rule of the Tsars with the Union of Soviet Socialist Republics.

BELOW Revolutionary movements throughout the world were marked by organized mass demonstrations such as those of the Nazi party at Nuremberg.

BELOW Benito Mussolini (1883–1945), founder of the Fascist movement in Italy.

ABOVE Pluto, God of the Underworld, sits in majesty, accompanied by Cerberus, the three-headed guardian of the infernal regions.

organizations which supply them with drugs, international terrorism, large-scale demonstrations, and the waves of mindless violence which so affect modern societies. Other symptoms of Pluto's influence are said to be atomic power, with its threat of bringing death to all mankind; the menace of economic depression as advanced nations struggle with balance-of-payments deficits and the Third World is burdened with unpayable debts and seemingly willfully hit with every conceivable disaster; minorities terrorizing majorities and causing mayhem out of all proportion to their numbers in their attempts to achieve independence or their other aims through violence; and civil wars inspired by conflicting ideologies.

Pluto makes everything worse or, in its positive aspects, better than usual, and this is true of any striking personality in whose horoscope its influence is prominent. His power for good or evil can be immense. The eccentric orbit of the planet is symbolic of the depths or heights to which mankind is capable of sinking or soaring.

But even at its worst Pluto is not destructive of hope. It destroys in order to build afresh and eliminates to clear the ground for renewal. From Pluto's realm comes Proserpine, the goddess of spring, hope and new life. In the individual

Pluto represents the limits of the mind's consciousness, and is concerned with that underworld in the depths of our psyche which is involved with the occult in its literal sense of "hidden." It is the planet of the parapsychological, sometimes of neuroses caused by dissociation, or discordances creating rebellion against the wholeness of the character.

In mundane matters Pluto's subject is an individualist, interested primarily in success in attaining his objects. If he has a home and family he will be staunchly faithful to them, but mainly because he needs a firm base from which to launch his career, and will therefore need a partner who is ready to subserve him in this.

Pluto's physiological domain is in the renewing of cells to replace those in the body that die, the reproductive functions in their widest sense, and the creative and regenerative processes.

Its symbol, a capital P combined with a capital L, represents the initials of Percival Lowell, who calculated Pluto's position before it was actually observed. To those who prefer a more esoteric meaning it can also represent the circle of the human mind connected to the level of the subconscious, or of the forces below even that, the universal subconscious which Jung postulated as uniting humankind at the deepest level.

BELOW Pluto carrying off Persephone: a detail from the Red-Figure Volute Krater, ornate Apulian style, c380–370 BC, by the Iliupersis Painter.

development of the sense of social responsibility. Libra is the ruler of the seventh house and strengthens this tendency. The sign is one of maturity and indicates that the change happens in the prime of life.

The influence of the Sun in Cancer (see **4.** above) is strengthened by its angular position.

Uranus in Cancer symbolizes the break with home and also the tendency of the subject for individual and original planning of her own home. Uranus deals with the occult and the spiritual and the third house with the ability to communicate with others, so the home might well contain a room set aside for a ministry of healing of body or spirit, or as a chapel or meditation room.

Mercury in Cancer strengthens the development of the retentive memory mentioned above, but also the tendency of the subject to be swayed by her emotions. This in turn could reinforce the disposition to subjectivity in judgment and prejudice in opinions which has already been mentioned. Cancer is the sign of the fourth house and its presence here shows the native's strong affection for her home, both as the family abode and as the material house.

7. Venus in Leo in the fifth house emphasizes the strong social sense of the subject. She loves entertaining. The combination of planet, sign and house here indicates an ardent and faithful lover and a loving mother of her children, but with a bent towards possessiveness and jealousy. Pluto is so far distant and slow moving that its influence on individual characters and lives is unobservable.

8. The individual aspects

(1) ☉☌☿ (good influence – benasp). This combination is one of power, vitality and liveliness of intellect.

(2) ☉♇♀ (bad influence – malasp). An aspect of minor significance, implying some emotional weakness that may result in certain unsatisfactory personal relationships.

(3) ☉□♃ and ☉□♆ (malasp). The T-squares of these three planets reinforce the danger of intolerance which appears in other parts of this horoscope. This is a characteristic due not so much to confidence in the rightness of the subject's opinions as to frustration and her vulnerability to the sufferings of the world. If her own life were to be unhappy, she could become morbidly sensitive to these miseries and furiously impatient with the failure of other people's efforts to solve the problems of mankind. Even with a secure background the intolerance arising out of her very idealism will never be far from the surface.

(4) ☉ ♅ (benasp). The markedly positive qualities of

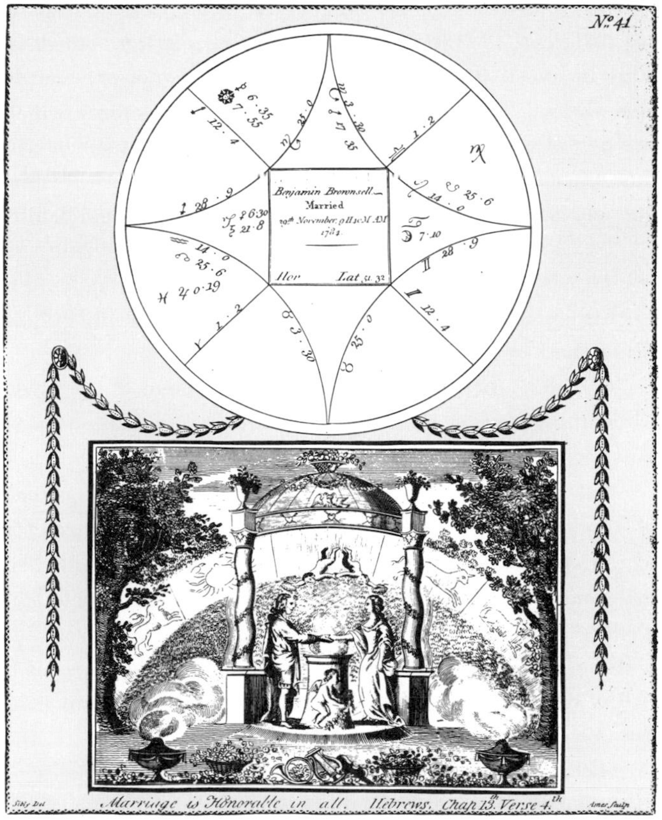

ABOVE Chart of a marriage in 1732 of an old, rich bridegroom to a young, poor bride, which E Sibley, an astrologer, phrophesied would fail. The bride left after one night.

the Sun are guided into unconventional paths by the influence of Uranus. Impatience with the status quo, though balanced by other elements in the chart, will always be present under the surface and the subject will take pride in thinking for herself.

(5) ☉ MC (malasp). As the MC symbolically stands for the summit or climax of the individual life and the powerful Sun is in opposition, this relationship suggests considerable struggles for the subject and possibly personal failure in the attainment of her aims.

(6) ☽✱♃ (benasp). The subject's affection for her family, cultivation of the spiritual side of her nature, disciplining of the faults of which she is conscious and attempts to attain spiritual maturity will go far to meet the weaknesses and handicaps of other aspects. The storms in her life can be met by a cultivation of "that peace which the world cannot give."

(7) ☽△♆ (benasp). This relationship reveals a mystical, intuitive streak in the character which is a good counterpoise to its outward vivacity, assertiveness and authority.

(8) ☽*♇ (benasp). The subject has the capacity to respond to conditions, to eliminate errors and to accept transformation. This means that she can discipline herself (not necessarily that she will!) against the impatience and intolerance which are part of her very idealism. It is likely that her instincts will guide her subconscious to know when she is at fault – it is the conscious facing up to shortcomings that may prove difficult.

(9) ☽* Ascendant (benasp). Early ideals will mature as life passes and not disappear. Cultivating and being faithful to them will help to lighten the darkness if the difficulties threatened by (3) and (5) above materialize.

(10) ☽π (benasp). This is a reinforcement of (9). Even when things are at their darkest there will be some joys to compensate.

(11) ☿□♃ and ☿□♆ (malasp). This is another pattern of T-squares and represents a gloomy side of the character which could surface if the subject's life were submitted to extreme tension. The strength and idealism of the intellect could give way to superficiality, extravagance of behaviour and opinion, or the finding of refuge in fantasy. Again there is a risk of despair caused by over-sensitivity to the sufferings of the world.

(12) ☿ ♂ ♅ (benasp). There is here a lively originality of thought, spiritual rather than intellectual.

(13) ☿ ⊻ ♇ (benasp). This is a slight confirmation of (8) where the instinct guides the subject in the direction of transformation and regeneration.

(14) ☿□ ascendant (malasp). There is an indication here of a parting of the ways, in that the beginning of life pointed in one direction whereas the subject developed along another, harder path.

(15) ☿□ MC (malasp). Once again there is a suggestion of struggle in that the subject's habits of thought will in some way conflict with the fulfillment of her aims.

(16) ♀ ⊻ ♄ (benasp). There is a tendency here to treat personal relationships cautiously – once bitten, twice shy? – but it is not strong.

(17) ♀ ♂ ♇ (benasp). Here the love and joy that are the properties of Venus are tinged with the elimination and transformation that are Pluto's domain. The subject has, through not always happy experience, learned to love truly.

(18) ♂□♄ (malasp). The assertiveness of Mars combines badly with Saturn's limitations to produce unhappy situations for the subject. This relationship could indicate a development in her of ideas which are unacceptable in the milieu in which she works, and which are suppressed or opposed by its more orthodox members.

(19) ♃□♅ (malasp). Another square! The optimism and expansiveness that are Jupiter's can be neutralized, once again by opposition aroused by the unconventional nature of the subject's thought.

(20) ♃♂♆ (malasp). Here Jupiter's "joviality" is once more countered, this time by the overwhelming sense of the world's miseries that Neptune can inspire in those who are over-sensitive to them.

(21) ♃⛣♇ (malasp). There is here a very slight influence of a consciousness of mortality that destroys joy, a sense of the pathos that underlies all life, perhaps doubt and self-distrust which the subject fights and mostly suppresses in herself.

(22) ♃ ♂ ascendant (benasp). The subject's natural disposition from the beginning of her life was optimistic and happy.

(23) ♃□ MC (malasp). Again there comes the element of frustration in the attainment of aims and fulfillment of ideals.

(24) ♅♂ MC (malasp). The unconventional streak in the subject again frustrates her.

(25) ♆♂ ascendant (malasp). Neptune, which in this horoscope has several times exposed the subject's sensitive nature to an overwhelming sense of the world's unhappiness, here directly conflicts with the strong influence of Jupiter's optimism at the beginning of her life. She has the weapon of innate happiness to fight the awareness of miseries about which she can do very little. Consequently she can steel herself against them without being overwhelmed by guilt. But depression may sometimes need to be fought hard.

(26) ♇△ asendant (benasp). Positive Pluto makes everything better. Here the planet of the end of things meets the subject's beginning. This suggests that at the end of her life, in spite of the struggles and frustrations, she will feel that having remained loyal to the truth as she sees it, she will have conquered – even if apparently frustrated in her aims.

Of the 28 aspects listed above (two each under 3 and 11) 14 include Uranus, Neptune and Pluto. In many personal horoscopes the interpreter would omit these references.

SUMMARY

We have here a well-balanced personality, innately happy and secure, with qualities of leadership that could inspire those who follow her. She is a good communicator in speech and writing. She possesses a lively, independent intellect, blessed with a good memory. This can develop strong, unconventional opinions which the subject will seek to propagate

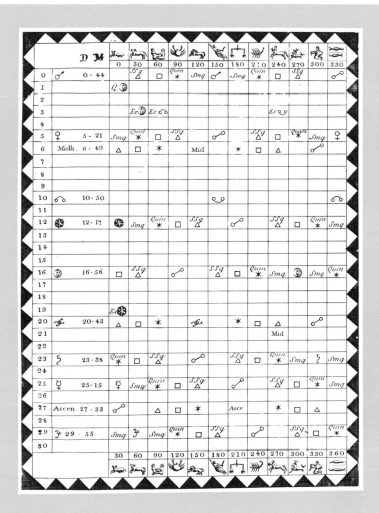

Table of aspects at the nativity of George Witchell, astronomer, born 21 March, 1728, from E Sibley's *Illustration of the Celestial Art of Astrology*, 1817.

energetically and which are likely to arouse opposition. Her case will not be helped by her impatience with what she might interpret as the lack of vision and imagination of her opponents and she risks being driven into tactlessness and intolerance in her presentation of what she is confident is right. She may be involved in considerable struggle and may well be frustrated in her ultimate aims. She must be careful to cultivate open-mindedness so as to appreciate the sincerity of those who oppose her, and not to react so strongly to criticism that she becomes entrenched in prejudice.

Another danger would appear to be financial. There is no hint of materialism in her chart and as one who has little interest in money she must avoid the danger of trusting inefficient or dishonest financial advisers. She needs to employ completely trustworthy counsellors in this field and avoid

speculation herself. Her emotions are powerful and her relationships on the whole happy, especially those within her close family. She is a homemaker, with a tendency to possessiveness – she may find it hard to let her children go when they reach an age at which they begin to think and plan for themselves. In wider circles she is sociable and enjoys communicating formally and informally.

There is considerable sensitivity to the sufferings of the world and a sense of guilt that she is secure and happy. Such sensitivity could make her extremely vulnerable if the circumstances of her own life should become unhappy.

Her mystical, intuitive streak which can express itself in religious activity or in mysteries more arcane. She is likely to feel, at the end of her life, whatever her successes or failures, that she has been true to herself and her ideals.

CHAPTER FIVE

A BRIEF HISTORY OF ASTROLOGY

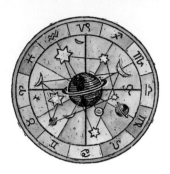

Astrology began over 5,000 and possibly as much as 7,000 years ago, the first exact science to be studied by mankind. It was, to begin with, a royal and national science. In Ur of the Chaldees, a city of Sumer, that part of Mesopotamia immediately north of the Persian Gulf where astrology was probably born, it was confined to divining the omens for king and nation only. North of Sumer was Babylonia and in those two countries were laid the foundations of the study from which the modern systems have descended.

The fixed constellations seemed unchanging, but in the clear atmosphere of Mesopotamia, where observation was assisted by wide expanses of flat landscape, the movement of those heavenly bodies which seemed to traverse regular paths

ABOVE An imaginary view of Babylon where, together with Sumer, the foundations of astrology were laid.

ABOVE On this cylinder seal of the Scribe Adda, *c*2400–2200 BC is pictured, among other deities, the Sun-God, Shamash (on the right).

LEFT A Chinese zodiacal vase of the 5th to 6th centuries AD decorated with the images of 12 animals representing the months of the year.

ABOVE A Babylonian boundary stone, *c*1120 BC, recording a gift of land, bears the symbols of gods invoked to protect the deed.

in the skies was noticed, and the planets we call Mercury, Venus, Mars, Jupiter and Saturn were known to the Sumerians, the Babylonians and their successors. The belt of the zodiac in which the paths of the planets mainly lay (though they occasionally wandered outside it, when they were thought to be resting in their "houses") may have been known for millenia, though most modern scholarship ascribes its recognition to Greek science of the sixth and fifth centuries BC. The Sumerians identified Venus with Innin or Inanna, the Lady of Heaven, and the Babylonians regarded her as Ishtar, goddess of war and carnage in her appearance as the Morning Star, but of love, procreation, fertility, gentleness and luxury when she shone as the Evening Star. She was the daughter of Sîn, the Moon god, and sister of Utu or Shamash, deity of the Sun. Nergal, god of war and destruction, and ruler of the underworld, was appropriately the red planet, Mars; Mercury was Babylonian Nabu; Jupiter was Marduk and Saturn Ninib.

Reports of earthly phenomena apparently resulting from the movements of heaven's gods, though most of them were on the level of meteorological forecasts, were recorded in writings known as the Enuma Anu Enlil tablets, dating from the beginning of the fourth millenium BC Records of predictions followed, first of events such as wars and floods, later birth horoscopes of individual kings, some of which still exist on cuneiform tablets.

Eastwards, Mesopotamian astrology penetrated to India around the sixth century BC and to China and Indo–China soon after (though there may have been some earlier influence).

Westwards it travelled to Egypt and Greece. Primitive peoples in western Europe, independently of Sumer and Babylon, had learned as early as 2000 BC to mark the solstices and other astronomical events by systems of megaliths. In Mexico, from about 300 AD, the Mayas developed an even more accurate knowledge of astronomy than the Babylonians, evolving a calendar of 365 days and a zodiac of thirteen signs. The Aztecs produced a somewhat cruder system.

LEFT A Mayan manuscript from Mexico. In the clear atmosphere of their location, the Mayas developed a sophisticated astronomical system.

MICHEL GAUQUELIN: A NEW PERSPECTIVE

Since his student days at the Sorbonne, when he studied psychology and statistics with research into astrology in mind, Gauquelin has devoted many years to the application of statistics to the science. In his *Astrology and Science* he built up a sufficiently powerful case against conventional astrology as to destroy it, but only, in a sense, to create it anew. For he discovered that a statistically significant proportion of 1,084 prominent medical academicians were born when either Mars or Saturn had just risen or were at their culmination. Later he confirmed by the examination of 25,000 celebrities in Germany, Italy, Belgium, Holland and France, and many thousands since, that irrespective of national culture and background, a man's profession corresponded to the positions of certain planets at his birth.

ciples have come to be recognized, the "observer effect" and the "sheep and goats effect." The former is the recognition that, except in the exact sciences (and perhaps not even there) there can be no such event as a completely objective experiment. This is because the observer, by the very act of observing, becomes part of the experiment and exerts an influence upon it. The latter describes the tendency of believers (sheep) in the possibility of, say, extrasensory perception, to score above chance in tests confirming its existence, whereas non-believers (goats) score at or below chance. It may be that only the faith of the subject and an empathy between him and the practitioner can release in the psychologically intuitive astrologer the ability to interpret correctly all the factors in the horoscope, and that this is the only "true" astrology

Gauquelin argues that our genetic code has stamped on it our youth, maturity and age, and predetermines particularly illnesses and accidents. The universe, including man, is subject to rhythms acting as cosmic "clocks" – can it be that the inner "clocks" of a human embryo predispose him to enter the world under certain cosmic conditions which correspond to his biological constitution, rather than that the planets influence him at birth? And that the parent's "clocks" determined conception?

Gauquelin further investigated "planetary heredity" by matching 15,000 parents and children, involving the examination of 300,000 positions of planets. He discovered a correlation between the birth skies of the parents and those of their children of which the probabilities against chance were

499,999 to one. The indications were clear for Mars, Jupiter, Saturn, the Moon and Venus. There was not enough evidence for Mercury, which is very small, nor for Uranus, Neptune and Pluto, which are very distant. The effects of hereditary characteristics were more marked in a child whose birth sky corresponded to that of his parents, but the results varied in the cases of births that were induced (as one would expect).

Writing on the birth data of his first sample of medical academicians, Gauquelin said, "Ordinary people *never* [my italics] showed this effect." What of people in limiting circumstances who could have become great doctors, given the opportunity? Or is Gauquelin to be taken literally? If he is, under what stars are "ordinary" people born?

Whatever future research may show, Gauquelin denies the thesis that planets govern professions or characters, suggesting only the biological clocks explanation. He seems not so much to have destroyed traditional astrology as to have turned it inside out. Instead of the heavens moulding the births of humans, the births have suited themselves to the heavens. Whatever the final results of research – if finality is reached before the stars have run their courses – it seems that at present an individual's belief, or not, in astrology depends on the "clocks" that determine his birthday and the planets that are where they are when he arrives.

Voyager I photograph of Saturn's moon Titan: if the planets affect us directly, sceptics claim, then why are the smaller celestial bodies ignored by astrologers in their calculations?

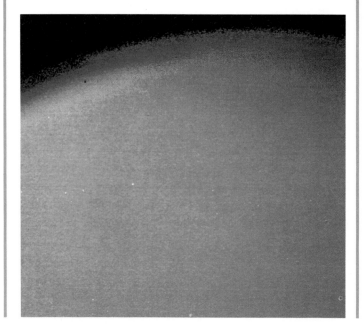

INDEX

BIBLIOGRAPHY

There are hundreds, even thousands, of books on astrology, from popular introductions to erudite and scholarly dissertations. The following list is not intended to be exhaustive but will serve as an introduction to the student to lead him on to still further reading.

COPE, LLOYD *Your Stars Are Numbered* Doubleday, New York, 1971

GAUQUELIN, MICHAEL *Astrology and Science* Mayflower Books, London, 1972

GOODMAN, LINDA *Sun Signs* Pan Books, London & Sydney. First Printing 1972, many reprintings since.

HEINDEL, MAX *Simplified Scientific Astrology* Melvin Powers, Wiltshire Book Company, Hollywood, California, 1989 (originally written 1928)

INNES, BRIAN *Horoscopes* Macdonald & Co., London, 1987

LEE, DAL *A Dictionary of Astrology* Sphere Books, London, 1969

MACLEOD, CHARLOTTE *Astrology for Sceptics* Turnstone Books, London, 1973

McINTOSH, CHRISTOPHER *Astrology* Macdonald Unit 75, London, 1970

The Astrologers and Their Creed Hutchinson, London, 1969

MAYO, JEFF *Teach Yourself Astrology* English Universities Press, London, 1964

The Astrologer's Astronomical Handbook Fowler, London, 1965

MICHELSON, NEIL F. *The American Ephemeris for the 20th Century 1900 to 2000, at Noon. Revised.* ACS Publications, San Diego, California, 1983.

The Koch Book of Tables ACS Publications, San Diego, California, Second Printing, 1987.

NAYLOR, P. I. H. *Astrology, an Historical Examination* Robert Maxwell, London, 1967.

RANDALL, SIDNEY *An ABC of the Old Science of Astrology* Foulsham and Co., London, 1917.

RUDHYAR, DANE *The Astrology of Personality* (2nd Edition) Servire, The Hague, 1963.

SHULMAN, SANDRA *An Encyclopedia of Astrology* Hamlyn, London, 1976.

THIERENS, A. E. *Elements of Esoteric Astrology* Rider & Co., London, 1931.

WEST, A. E. AND TOONDER, J. G. *The Case for Astrology* Macdonald, London, 1973.

WOODRUFF, BOB *Astrology for Fun* Tarnhelm Press Lakemont, Georgia, 1976.

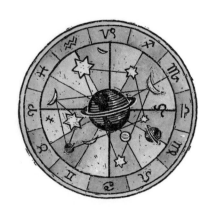